C000297828

SPIRIT WRITER

Understanding this Journey Called Life: A
Guide to Navigating Life's Challenges

Wendy Sheffield

Spiritwriterspeaks

Previous publications include:

Spirit Writer (Book 1)
Pure Spirit (Book 2)
Spirit Healer (Book 3)
The Final Awakening Of A Natural Medium (Book 4)

Spirit Writer (Books 1-4) A Journey of Spiritual Awakening and
Self-Discovery

The Devil Within: Evil In This World Today

All rights reserved
Copyright © Wendy Sheffield 2024
AKA SPIRITWRITERSPEAKS

The right of Wendy Sheffield to be identified as the author of
this work has been asserted in accordance with Section 78 of
the Copyright, Designs and Patents Act 1988.

Cover image copyright to unsplash.com licence via Coverjig
Designed by Author: Wendy Sheffield

This book is published by SPIRITWRITERSPEAKS

This book is sold subject to the conditions that it shall not, by
way of trade or otherwise, be leant, resold, hired out or
otherwise circulated without the author's or publisher's prior
consent in any form of binding or cover other than that in which
it is published snd without a similar condition including this
condition being imposed on the subsequent purchaser.

A CIP record for this book is available from the British Library.

❀ Created with Vellum

Thank you to my spirit guides. May they continue to guide me so that I can guide others!

"The journey of life is not about reaching the destination, but about embracing the detours, conquering the challenges, and treasuring the moments along the way"

"Life is not just about the destination, but the beauty lies in the journey itself"

Contents

Understanding This Journey Called Life

"Life becomes simpler and more meaningful when we embrace the beauty of understanding rather than seeking constant answers"

When we start our life we are not aware of what lies ahead...

Life is a journey that each one of us embarks on from the moment we are born. It is a journey filled with ups and downs, successes and failures, joy and sorrow. Understanding this journey called life is essential in order to navigate through it with grace and purpose.

The aim of this book is to help you navigate this journey. There will always be various challengers to face in life. We have tackled only a handful of potential challenges that anyone can experience in life, but we hope that our readers will understand the overall message contained therein.

Understanding This Journey Called Life

Life is often compared to a rollercoaster ride, with its twists and turns, ups and downs. It is a journey filled with challenges and obstacles that test our strength and resilience. It is during these difficult moments that we learn the most about ourselves and our true potential. It is through adversity that we grow and develop as individuals.

But life is not just about overcoming challenges, it is also about finding happiness and fulfilment. It is about discovering our passions and pursuing them with zeal and enthusiasm. It is about creating meaningful connections and building lasting relationships. It is about finding balance in our lives and taking care of our physical, emotional, and spiritual well-being.

Understanding this journey called *life* means having a clear sense of purpose and direction. It means knowing what truly matters to us and aligning our actions and decisions with our values and beliefs. It means setting goals and working towards them with determination and perseverance. It means embracing change and embracing the unknown, knowing that it is through these experiences that we discover new possibilities and opportunities.

Life is also about embracing the present moment and making the most of each and every day. It is about living in the here and now, instead of dwelling on the past or worrying about the future.

It is about finding joy and gratitude in the simple things and appreciating the beauty that surrounds us.

Let's now tackle potential challenges (with spirit's guidance) that can be experienced throughout someone's life...

Chapter 1
Spirit's message on the Journey of Life

Many people have many different thoughts.

Many people only listen to their own thoughts; understanding them isn't always easy.

When there's understanding, there's happiness and no sadness.

We should realise we're not alone.

Spirit sends love to us and words that are needed. When we're all aware, people will understand.

The knowledge comes down to everyone who's ready to receive it. Some people may question spirit intelligence, but the knowledge only comes to those that are ready for it.

Ask, and the true meaning of love will come to us, and then everyone will be together as one.

We'll be one voice, with no separation of language. We'll understand each other.

When people work together and stand together, they won't

stand apart, and everyone will share the love.

Stop and listen. Stop and share!

> — This message was channelled by the Author, Wendy Sheffield, at the time she wrote her second book *Pure Spirit*.

Chapter 2
Importance of positivity in life

"Positivity is not just a state of mind, but a powerful force that can transform your life and inspire those around you"

Positivity is a state of mind that plays a crucial role in shaping our lives. It is the ability to maintain a positive outlook, even in the face of challenges and adversities. The importance of positivity in life cannot be overstated, as it has a profound impact on our mental, emotional, and physical well-being.

Firstly, positivity cultivates a healthy mindset. When we think positively, we are more likely to have a greater sense of self-worth, optimism, and resilience. This enables us to navigate through life's ups and downs with grace and strength. Positive thoughts also have the power to attract positive outcomes. When we believe in ourselves and our abilities, we are more likely to achieve our goals and dreams.

Secondly, positivity enhances our overall well-being. Research has shown that individuals with a positive outlook on life tend to have better physical health, lower levels of stress, and improved immune function. Positive emotions such as joy, gratitude, and love have been scientifically proven to boost our immune system, reduce pain, and promote overall wellness. Moreover, positive thinking is also linked to better cardiovascular health and increased longevity.

Furthermore, positivity has a ripple effect on our relationships and social interactions. When we approach others with a positive attitude, it creates harmony and a sense of goodwill. Positivity fosters empathy, understanding, and compassion, leading to stronger and more fulfilling connections with others. It also creates an uplifting atmosphere, where people feel motivated, supported, and encouraged to be their best selves.

In addition, positivity is essential for personal growth and success. When we embrace a positive mindset, it allows us to see opportunities where others see obstacles. It fuels our motivation and determination to overcome challenges and persevere in the pursuit of our goals. Positive individuals are more likely to take risks, step out of their comfort zones, and seize opportunities for personal and professional growth.

In conclusion, positivity is a powerful force that has the ability to transform our lives for the better. It enables us to face life's challenges with strength and resilience, promotes our physical and mental well-being, enhances our relationships, and fuels our personal growth and success. Cultivating positivity is a lifelong journey that requires conscious effort and practice. By choosing to focus on the positive aspects of life and maintaining a positive attitude, we can create a life filled with joy, fulfilment, and success.

Chapter 3
Facing challenges

"Life challenges are not meant to break you, but to mould you into the person you were always meant to be"

Life is a journey filled with ups and downs, and along the way, we are bound to face numerous challenges. These challenges come in various forms and can have a significant impact on our lives. They test our resilience, character, and determination to overcome obstacles. While the exact challenges that each individual will face differ, there are some common struggles that we are likely to encounter.

One of the most common challenges in life is facing failure. Whether it is in academics, career, relationships, or personal goals, failure can be a demoralising experience. It tests our ability to bounce back, learn from our mistakes, and try again. Overcoming failure requires perseverance and a positive mindset to keep moving forward despite setbacks.

Another challenge we often face is dealing with change. Life is constantly evolving, and we must adapt to new situations and circumstances. This can be challenging, especially when it involves leaving our comfort zones or facing uncertainty. It requires a flexible mindset, open to embracing new experiences and learning from them.

In addition to failure and change, we also encounter the challenge of managing relationships. Whether it is with friends, family, or romantic partners, relationships can be complex and require effort and compromise. Navigating through conflicts, disagreements, and differences in opinions can be difficult, and maintaining healthy relationships requires effective communication and understanding.

Furthermore, mental and emotional challenges are becoming increasingly prevalent in today's society. Many individuals struggle with anxiety, depression, stress, or self-doubt. These challenges can affect all aspects of life, including personal relationships, work, and overall well-being. Overcoming mental and emotional obstacles often requires seeking support from professionals or loved ones and implementing coping mechanisms and self-care practices.

Lastly, societal challenges also play a significant role in our lives. Issues such as poverty, discrimination, inequality, and environmental concerns can have a profound impact on individuals and communities. Overcoming these challenges requires collective efforts, awareness, and a strong sense of social responsibility.

In conclusion, life is filled with challenges that shape who we are as individuals. Failure, change, relationships, mental and emotional struggles, and societal issues are just a few of the hurdles we may encounter. However, it is through these challenges that we grow and develop resilience, determination, and empathy. By facing these obstacles head-on and learning from them, we can evolve into stronger, more compassionate individuals.

Chapter 4
Facing failure

"Failure is not a stumbling block on the road to success, but rather a stepping stone that inspires resilience and fuels determination"

Failure is an inevitable part of life. It is something that everyone experiences at some point, and it often serves as a stepping stone to ultimate success. While failure may be disheartening and discouraging, it is important to remember that it is not the end of the road. In fact, it is often through failure that we learn the most valuable lessons and discover our true potential.

One of the most significant lessons that failure teaches us is the importance of perseverance. When we face failure, it is easy to become discouraged and give up on our dreams. However, it is crucial to remember that success rarely comes without its fair share of setbacks. It is through our ability to pick ourselves up and keep pushing forward that we prove our determination and commitment to achieving our goals.

Moreover, failure provides us with an opportunity for self-reflection and growth. When we fail, we are forced to examine what went wrong and what we can do differently in the future. This process of introspection allows us to identify our weaknesses and areas for improvement. It is through this growth and development that we become more resilient and better equipped to handle future challenges.

Failure also teaches us the value of humility. When we experience success after success, it is easy to become complacent and arrogant. However, failure has a way of humbling us and reminding us that we are not infallible. This humbling experience can be a catalyst for personal growth and the development of important character traits such as empathy, compassion, and gratitude.

Perhaps most importantly, failure teaches us the importance of resilience and the ability to bounce back. Life is full of ups and downs, and it is our ability to weather the storms that defines our character and determines our success. Instead of letting failure defeat us, we must use it as an opportunity to reassess our goals, create new strategies, and move forward with renewed determination.

In conclusion, failure is not something to be feared or avoided, but rather embraced as a necessary part of the journey towards success. It is through failure that we learn valuable lessons, develop important character traits, and ultimately grow into the best versions of ourselves. So, the next time you face failure, remember that it is not the end, but rather the beginning of a new and improved chapter in your life.

Chapter 5
Dealing with change

"Change is not always easy, but it is necessary for growth and progress in life"

Change is an inevitable part of life. Whether it is small changes in our daily routines or major life-altering events, we are constantly faced with the need to adapt and adjust. However, dealing with change can be a challenging task for many individuals. Some people find it difficult to let go of the familiar and embrace the unknown, while others may fear the potential consequences that change may bring. Nevertheless, it is important to recognise that change is essential for personal growth and development.

One of the biggest obstacles in dealing with change is the fear of the unknown. Human beings have a natural tendency to seek comfort and security in stability, and any disruption to this stability can be unsettling. This fear often stems from the uncertainty and unpredictability that change brings. However, it is important to remember that change can also bring new opportunities and possibilities. By embracing change and stepping outside of our comfort zones, we open ourselves up to new experiences and opportunities for growth.

Another challenge in dealing with change is the resistance to let go of the familiar. We become accustomed to our routines and habits, and any deviation from these can be met with resistance. However, clinging to the familiar can prevent us from experiencing personal growth and hinder our ability to adapt to new situations. In order to effectively deal with change, it is crucial to let go of the past and embrace the present moment. This can be achieved through self-reflection and mindfulness, allowing us to fully accept and appreciate the changes that come our way.

Furthermore, the fear of failure often accompanies change. We may worry about the potential negative outcomes or the possibility of not being able to handle the new situation. However, it is important to recognise that failure is simply a stepping stone towards success. Every change brings with it the opportunity to learn and grow, and even if we stumble along the way, we can use these experiences as valuable lessons for the future.

In conclusion, dealing with change is an essential skill for personal growth and development. By embracing change and letting go of the familiar, we open ourselves up to new experiences and opportunities. It is important to overcome the fear of the unknown and the resistance to let go, and instead approach change with an open mind and a willingness to learn. By doing so, we can navigate through life's ups and downs with grace and resilience.

Chapter 6
Managing relationships

"Relationships are like flowers, they require nurturing, communication and patience. When given the right amount of care, they bloom into beautiful connections that enrich our lives"

Relationships are an integral part of our lives and play a crucial role in shaping our overall well-being and happiness. Whether it is our family, friends, colleagues, or romantic partners, maintaining healthy and strong relationships is essential for a fulfilling life. However, managing relationships can be a complex task that requires effort, under-standing, and effective communication.

One of the key aspects of managing relationships is effective communication. Clear and open commu-nication is vital for resolving conflicts, expressing emotions, and understanding each other's needs and desires. Active listening and expressing oneself honestly and respectfully are essential skills that help in fostering trust and deepening connections. By actively listening to others and understanding their perspectives, we can avoid misunderstandings and enhance emotional intimacy in our relationships.

Another important aspect of managing relationships is setting boundaries. Each person has their own individual needs, and it is crucial to communicate and establish boundaries to ensure that these needs are respected. Boundaries help maintain a sense of individuality and prevent the feeling of being overwhelmed or taken for granted in a relationship. By setting clear boundaries, we can create a healthy balance between giving and receiving in our relationships.

Furthermore, managing relationships requires empathy and understanding. Each person is unique, with their own experiences, emotions, and perspectives. It is important to be empathetic and try to understand the other person's point of view without judgment. Showing empathy and validating one another's feelings helps in building a strong emotional connection and fosters a sense of trust and support in the relationship.

Additionally, managing relationships involves compromise and collaboration. No two individuals are alike, and conflicts and differences are inevitable in any relationship. It is essential to be flexible and willing to compromise to find mutually satisfactory solutions. Collaboration involves working together as a team, respecting each other's opinions, and finding common ground. By fostering collaboration, we can navigate conflicts and challenges effectively, ensuring that the relationship remains healthy and fulfilling.

In conclusion, managing relationships is a lifelong endeavour that requires effort, understanding, and effective communication. By cultivating skills such as effective communication, setting boundaries, empathy, and collaboration, we can build and maintain strong, healthy, and fulfilling relationships. Investing time and energy into managing relationships is an investment in our overall well-being and happiness. As the saying goes, "No man is an island," and nurturing our relationships is vital for a meaningful and balanced life.

Chapter 7

Coping with mental and emotional challenges

"Strength doesn't come from avoiding our mental and emotional changes, but from embracing them and rising above them"

Throughout our lives, we all face various mental and emotional challenges. Whether it's the loss of a loved one, job stress, relationship issues, or personal insecurities, these challenges can take a toll on our well-being. Coping with these challenges is crucial for our mental and emotional health, allowing us to navigate through life's ups and downs with resilience and strength.

One of the first steps in coping with mental and emotional challenges is to acknowledge and accept our emotions. It's important to give ourselves permission to feel sad, angry, or anxious, as denying these emotions can lead to further distress. By allowing ourselves to experience these emotions, we can begin to process and understand them.

Another important coping mechanism is seeking support from others. Whether it's talking to a trusted friend or family member, seeking professional help from a therapist, or joining a support group, having someone to listen and offer guidance can be instrumental in overcoming challenges. It's essential to remember that we don't have to face our difficulties alone, and reaching out for help is a sign of strength, not weakness.

Additionally, engaging in self-care practices is crucial when facing mental and emotional challenges. Taking care of ourselves physically, emotionally, and spiritually can provide a solid foundation for coping with difficulties. This can include activities such as practicing mindfulness or meditation, exercising regularly, eating a nutritious diet, getting adequate sleep, and exploring hobbies and interests. These actions nourish our minds and bodies, providing us with the resilience and strength needed to face challenges head-on.

Developing healthy coping strategies and skills is also essential for managing mental and emotional challenges. This can include techniques such as deep breathing, practicing positive self-talk, journaling, or engaging in creative outlets such as art or music. By incorporating these strategies into our daily lives, we can better regulate our emotions and reduce stress levels.

Lastly, it's important to maintain a positive mindset and cultivate gratitude. Focusing on the positives in life, no matter how small, can help shift our perspective and foster resilience. Cultivating gratitude through practices such as keeping a gratitude journal or expressing gratitude to others can also have a profound impact on our overall well-being.

In conclusion, coping with mental and emotional challenges is an ongoing process that requires self-awareness, support, self-care, healthy coping strategies, and a positive mindset. By acknowledging our emotions, seeking support, practicing self-care, developing healthy coping skills, and cultivating gratitude, we can navigate through life's challenges with resilience and strength. It's important to remember that we are not alone in our struggles, and there is always hope for a brighter future.

Chapter 8
Coping with societal challenges

"Adaptability is the key to not just surviving, but thriving amidst societal changes in life"

In life, we often come across various challenges, and one of the biggest challenges we face is coping with societal issues. These challenges can range from discrimination, inequality, poverty, and many more. It is essential for us to acknowledge and address these challenges in order to create a better society.

Discrimination is a prevalent issue in our society, be it based on race, gender, religion, or caste. It is disheartening to see individuals being judged and mistreated solely based on these factors. Coping with discrimination can be tough, as it affects one's self-esteem and confidence. However, it is crucial for us to stand up against discrimination and promote inclusivity and acceptance. By educating ourselves and others about the importance of equality, we can create a more tolerant society.

Another societal challenge that many face is poverty. Poverty not only affects individuals economically but also has a profound impact on their mental and emotional well-being. Coping with poverty requires not only support from the government but also collective efforts from society. By addressing the root causes of poverty, such as lack of education and job opportunities, and providing assistance and resources to those in need, we can work towards eliminating poverty and promoting social equality.

Inequality is another challenge that we need to cope with in society. Whether it is income inequality or gender inequality, it is important to ensure that everyone has equal opportunities and rights. Coping with inequality involves advocating for equal rights and opportunities, promoting education and awareness, and challenging societal norms that perpetuate inequality.

Coping with societal challenges can be difficult, but it is crucial for us to have a positive mindset and work towards finding solutions. By promoting compassion, empathy, and understanding, we can create a society that is inclusive and supportive of all its members. Additionally, it is important for us to educate ourselves and others about these challenges and actively contribute to the betterment of society.

In conclusion, coping with societal challenges is an integral part of life. Whether it is discrimination, poverty, or inequality, it is essential for us to acknowledge these challenges and work towards finding solutions. By standing up against discrimination, advocating for equal rights, and promoting compassion and understanding, we can create a society that is more inclusive and supportive for all. Let us strive towards creating a better society for ourselves and future generations.

Chapter 9
What does God mean to you?

"God is the infinite of love, strength, and guidance that resides within the depths of your being, reminding you of my true purpose and providing solace in the midst of life's challenges"

The concept of God is a deeply personal and individualistic one. Each individual interprets and understands the meaning of God in their own unique way. For some, God represents an omnipotent and omniscient being who guides and provides solace in times of need. For others, God is a symbol of hope, faith, and strength. The meaning of God varies from person to person, depending on their belief system, upbringing, and life experiences.

To me, God is the embodiment of love, compassion, and wisdom. I see God as a guiding force that helps me navigate through life's challenges and uncertainties. God is the source of my inner strength and the voice of conscience that guides me towards making ethical and moral choices. Through prayer and meditation, I connect with God and seek guidance, comfort, and peace.

God is also the source of inspiration and creativity. As a writer, I often turn to God for inspiration and guidance in my creative pursuits. I believe that God is the ultimate source of all knowledge and creativity, and by tapping into this divine energy, I am able to produce my best work.

Additionally, God serves as a source of comfort and solace during times of grief and sorrow. When faced with the loss of a loved one or personal hardships, I find solace in knowing that God is with me, offering support and understanding. The belief in a higher power provides comfort and reassurance that there is a greater plan at work, even in the midst of pain and suffering.

Furthermore, God represents a sense of unity and interconnectedness. I believe that we are all part of a larger cosmic plan, interconnected with each other and the universe. God is the unifying force that brings people together, encourages compassion and empathy, and fosters a sense of belonging and unity among all beings.

In conclusion, the meaning of God varies for each individual. To me, God represents love, compassion, guidance, inspiration, comfort, and unity. God is a deeply personal and transcendent force that helps me navigate through life's joys and challenges, provide inspiration and creativity, offer solace in times of grief, and foster a sense of unity and interconnectedness with all beings.

The message is clear from this chapter, find God in your own way...

Chapter 10

You are in control of your own destiny

"Your destiny is not determined by chance, but by the choices you make and the actions you take"

In life, there are countless decisions that we have to make. From the moment we wake up to the time we go to bed, we are constantly faced with choices that shape our destiny. Some may argue that fate plays a significant role in determining our path, but I firmly believe that we are in control of our own destiny.

Being in control of our destiny means taking responsibility for our actions and making conscious decisions that align with our goals and aspirations. It means not being influenced by external factors or succumbing to societal pressures. It means having the courage to stand up for what we believe in and pursue our passions, regardless of what others may think.

One of the most important aspects of being in control of our own destiny is setting goals. Without goals, we are like ships without a compass, drifting aimlessly in the vast ocean of life. Goals give us direction and purpose. They motivate us to push ourselves and strive for excellence. Whether it's achieving a certain career milestone, starting a family, or travelling the world, setting goals allows us to take control of our own destiny and shape our future.

Furthermore, being in control of our own destiny requires us to embrace opportunities and take risks. Life is full of uncertainties, and it's easy to succumb to fear and play it safe. However, it is through taking risks that we discover our true potential and achieve greatness. Whether it's starting a business, pursuing a new hobby, or embarking on a new adventure, taking risks opens doors to endless possibilities and allows us to create our own destiny.

Another crucial aspect of being in control of our own destiny is resilience. Life is not always smooth sailing, and we will undoubtedly face obstacles and setbacks along the way. However, it is during these challenging times that our true character is revealed. Being resilient means bouncing back from failure, learning from our mistakes, and persevering in the face of adversity. It means never giving up and staying committed to our dreams and aspirations, regardless of the obstacles that come our way.

In conclusion, being in control of our own destiny empowers us to shape our future and live a life of purpose and fulfilment. It requires setting goals, embracing opportunities, taking risks, and being resilient in the face of adversity. It is through our actions and decisions that we pave the way for a brighter tomorrow. So, let us seize the reins of our destiny and make the most of the precious gift of life.

Chapter 11

Believe In Your Dreams!

"Believe in your dreams, for they are the whispers of your soul reminding you of the incredible potential that lies within you"

Dreams are powerful. They have the ability to ignite a fire within us, to spur us on towards greatness. Throughout history, countless individuals have achieved remarkable success by simply believing in their dreams and pursuing them relentlessly, despite all odds. In a world that often tries to crush dreams and discourage individuals from reaching their full potential, it is crucial for us to hold on to our dreams and never give up!

Believing in our dreams is not always an easy journey. There will be obstacles, setbacks, and moments of self-doubt along the way. However, it is during these times that our belief in our dreams becomes even more vital. It is during these times that we must remind ourselves of the passion, determination, and purpose that lie behind our dreams. It is during these times that we must gather our strength and press on, knowing that our dreams are worth fighting for.

One of the greatest examples of someone who believed in his dreams against all odds is the famous scientist, Thomas Edison. Despite facing numerous failures and setbacks in his attempts to invent the electric light bulb, Edison never gave up. Instead, he viewed each failure as a lesson and an opportunity to learn and grow. It was Edison's unwavering belief in his dreams that eventually led to his successful invention and forever changed the world.

Similarly, another iconic figure who believed in her dreams is Oprah Winfrey. Born into poverty and facing numerous challenges throughout her life, Oprah could have easily succumbed to the difficulties and settled for a mediocre existence. However, she dared to dream big and persevered through adversity. Today, Oprah is one of the most influential and successful people in the world, inspiring millions with her story of resilience and determination.

Believing in our dreams is not only about achieving personal success; it is also about fulfilling our purpose in life. Each of us has unique gifts and talents that, when embraced and nurtured, have the potential to make a profound impact on the world. By believing in our dreams, we give ourselves the opportunity to step into our true potential and make a meaningful difference in the lives of others.

In conclusion, believing in our dreams is a powerful force that can propel us towards greatness. It is during times of adversity and self-doubt that our belief in our dreams becomes even more important. Like Thomas Edison and Oprah Winfrey, we must never give up on our dreams and continue to pursue them relentlessly. By doing so, we not only achieve personal success but also fulfil our purpose in life and make a positive impact on the world. So, let us hold on to our dreams, believe in ourselves, and never stop striving towards our highest aspirations.

Remember, it was the author's dream which led her to discover who she was!

Chapter 12
Coping with Grief

"Grief is not a sign of weakness, but a testament to the depth of love shared. Embrace it, process it, and allow yourself to heal"

Coping with grief is an inevitable part of the human experience. At some point in our lives, we all encounter loss and must navigate the difficult process of grieving. Whether it be the loss of a loved one, the end of a relationship, or the death of a pet, grief can be overwhelming and all-consuming. However, it is important to remember that grieving is a natural and necessary process that allows us to heal and move forward.

There is no right or wrong way to grieve. Each individual will have their own unique experience and timeline for healing. It is important to allow yourself the time and space to process your emotions and to be gentle with yourself along the way. Surround yourself with a support system of friends and family who can provide comfort and understanding during this difficult time.

One of the most important aspects of coping with grief is acknowledging and expressing your emotions. It is crucial to allow yourself to feel and express your sadness, anger, and confusion. Bottling up your emotions will only prolong the healing process and may lead to further emotional distress down the road. Find healthy outlets for your emotions, such as talking to a trusted friend or family member, journaling, or participating in a physical activity that allows you to release pent-up emotions.

Self-care is also crucial when coping with grief. Take the time to care for yourself both physically and emotionally. Engage in activities that bring you joy and provide a sense of normalcy. This can include exercise, spending time in nature, engaging in hobbies, or seeking professional help through therapy or counselling.

Grief can also be an opportunity for personal growth and reflection. Take the time to reflect on the memories and lessons that the loss has brought into your life. Celebrate the life and impact of your loved one and find ways to honour their memory.

Lastly, be patient with yourself. Grief is a process that takes time, and healing does not happen overnight. It is important to be gentle with yourself and allow yourself to fully experience and accept your emotions. Remember that everyone copes with grief differently, and there is no right or wrong way to navigate through this difficult time.

In conclusion, coping with grief is an essential part of the human experience. It is crucial to acknowledge and express your emotions, surround yourself with a supportive network, practice self-care, and be patient with yourself throughout the healing process. Remember that grief is a personal journey, and there is no timeline for healing.

Chapter 13
Coping With Loneliness

"Loneliness is not a reflection of our worth, but an invitation to discover the incredible strength and connection that lies within us"

Loneliness is a universal human emotion that everyone experiences at some point in their lives. It can be a distressing feeling, making individuals feel isolated and disconnected from others. Coping with loneliness requires a combination of self-reflection, seeking social support, and cultivating meaningful connections.

To begin with, self-reflection is crucial in understanding the root causes of loneliness and finding ways to address them. It is important to ask oneself why you are feeling lonely. Is it due to a lack of social interaction, a recent breakup or loss, or a feeling of not belonging? Once the underlying causes are identified, individuals can take steps to change their situation. This may involve engaging in activities that bring joy and fulfilment, such as pursuing hobbies or volunteering. Developing a sense of purpose and meaning can help alleviate feelings of loneliness.

Furthermore, seeking social support is essential in coping with loneliness. Humans are social creatures by nature, and we thrive on connections with others. Sharing our experiences and emotions can provide comfort and understanding. This can be achieved by reaching out to family and friends, joining support groups, or even seeking therapy. Connection and companionship play a vital role in combating loneliness, as they provide a sense of belonging and support.

Additionally, cultivating meaningful connections is crucial in coping with loneliness. Meaningful connections are built on mutual trust, respect, and shared values. Engaging in activities or communities that align with one's interests and values can facilitate the formation of these connections. This can include joining clubs, participating in group activities, or attending social events. By surrounding oneself with like-minded individuals, one can foster friendships and create a support network.

In conclusion, coping with loneliness requires a multi-faceted approach that involves self-reflection, seeking social support, and cultivating meaningful connections. Through self-reflection, individuals can identify the root causes of their loneliness and take steps to address them. Seeking social support provides comfort and understanding, while cultivating meaningful connections helps foster a sense of belonging and support. Loneliness is a temporary state that can be overcome with self-awareness and proactive efforts to connect with others.

Chapter 14
Coping With Jealousy

"Jealousy is a reflection of our own insecurities, not a measure of someone else's success"

Jealousy is a complex emotion that can often consume a person's thoughts and actions. It stems from a deep-seated feeling of insecurity or fear of losing something or someone significant. Coping with jealousy is crucial for personal growth and maintaining healthy relationships.

The first step in tackling jealousy is self-reflection. One must identify the root cause of their jealousy and understand why you feel threatened or insecure. This introspection allows individuals to gain a better understanding of their emotions and take steps towards addressing them.

An essential aspect of coping with jealousy is building self-esteem and self-confidence. Often, jealousy arises from a lack of belief in oneself and comparing oneself to others. By focusing on personal accomplishments and recognising one's unique qualities, individuals can develop a sense of self-worth and reduce feelings of envy.

Another helpful approach to overcoming jealousy is practicing gratitude. By appreciating and acknowledging the blessings in one's life, individuals become more content and less focused on what others have. Developing a gratitude mindset shifts the focus from scarcity to abundance, leading to a more positive outlook on life.

Open and honest communication is paramount when dealing with jealousy in relationships. It is crucial to express one's feelings, concerns, and insecurities to their partner or loved ones instead of letting jealousy fester and damage the relationship. Healthy communication allows for understanding, empathy, and finding solutions together.

Developing a sense of trust is fundamental in coping with jealousy. Trusting oneself and trusting others form the foundation of any relationship. It requires being secure in one's self-worth and believing that others will act in a trustworthy manner. By cultivating trust, individuals can relinquish their grip on jealousy and foster healthy relationships.

Mindfulness and focusing on the present moment can also help individuals cope with jealousy. Rather than dwelling on what others have or comparing oneself to them, living in the present allows individuals to appreciate their own journey and progress. This mindfulness practice promotes self-acceptance and reduces envy.

Lastly, seeking support from friends, family, or a therapist can be beneficial in navigating through jealousy. Sharing one's struggles with trusted individuals can provide valuable insights, advice, and emotional support. Surrounding oneself with a supportive network can alleviate feelings of jealousy and provide a sense of belonging.

In conclusion, coping with jealousy requires self-reflection, building self-esteem, practicing gratitude, open communication, developing trust, mindfulness, and seeking support. By employing these strategies, individuals can overcome jealousy and lead happier, more fulfilling lives. It is a journey of self-discovery and growth that ultimately leads to personal and interpersonal satisfaction.

Chapter 15
Understanding Greed

"Greed blinds us to the abundance around us, leaving us constantly hungry for more, and forever unsatisfied"

Greed is a universal human characteristic that has been present throughout history and across cultures. It is often defined as an intense desire for wealth, power, or possessions. Greed is often seen as a negative trait, as it can lead people to prioritise their own desires over the needs of others and can result in harmful actions. However, it is important to understand the underlying reasons behind greed in order to address its root causes and find ways to mitigate its impact on society.

One possible explanation for greed is the innate survival instinct that is ingrained in human nature. From an evolutionary perspective, the desire to accumulate resources is seen as a means of ensuring one's own survival and the survival of their offspring. In this sense, greed can be viewed as a natural response to the scarcity of resources and the fear of deprivation.

In addition to survival instincts, societal factors also contribute to the development of greed. The emphasis placed on material wealth and success in many societies can lead individuals to prioritise the acquisition of wealth and possessions above all else. The constant exposure to advertisements and media that promote a consumerist lifestyle further exacerbates this desire for more.

Furthermore, the culture of competition and individualism that is prevalent in many societies also fuels greed. The belief that one must constantly strive to be better than others and accumulate more wealth and possessions than the next person can create a sense of never-ending desire for more. In such a competitive environment, individuals may feel the need to amass as much as they can in order to secure their own position and status.

While greed can have negative consequences, it is important to recognise that not all forms of ambition or desire for wealth are inherently bad. In fact, it is often through the pursuit of personal goals and aspirations that great achievements and advancements are made in society. The key lies in finding a balance between personal ambition and the well-being of others.

In conclusion, greed is a complex human trait that can be influenced by both innate survival instincts and societal factors. While greed can lead to harmful actions and a disregard for others, it is important to recognise that not all ambition or desire for wealth is negative. By understanding the underlying causes of greed and promoting a more balanced approach to personal success, we can work towards a society that prioritises the well-being of all its members. Greed is a complex and multifaceted human emotion that has been a topic of philosophical and psychological inquiry for centuries. It is commonly defined as an intense and insatiable desire for more wealth, power, or possessions than one actually needs. While greed is often associated with negative connotations, it is important to understand its origins, implications, and potential for both positive and negative outcomes.

Chapter 16
Personal Growth

"The true measure of success lies not in what we
achieve externally, but in personal growth we
experience from within"

Personal growth is an essential aspect of every
individual's life. It is the process of self-improvement and self-development, which involves setting
and achieving personal goals, embracing new experiences, and continuously learning. The value of
personal growth lies in its ability to shape us into
better versions of ourselves, allowing us to reach
our full potential and live a fulfilling life.

One of the key reasons why personal growth is
important is because it enables us to become more
self-aware. Through self-reflection and introspection, we gain a deeper understanding of our
strengths, weaknesses, and values. This self-
awareness is crucial in making informed decisions

and taking actions that are aligned with our authentic selves. As we become more attuned to our true aspirations and desires, we are empowered to pursue meaningful goals and create a life that is in accordance with our values.

Furthermore, personal growth allows us to develop essential life skills. Whether it is communication skills, time management, or problem-solving abilities, personal growth enables us to acquire and refine these skills, which are invaluable in both personal and professional settings. By continuously learning and expanding our knowledge, we become adaptable and resilient in the face of challenges. This, in turn, enhances our employability and opens up doors for new opportunities.

In addition to these practical benefits, personal growth also plays a significant role in our emotional well-being. As we work towards personal goals and witness our progress, we experience a sense of accomplishment and fulfilment. This boosts our self-esteem and self-confidence, fostering a positive mindset and improving our overall mental health. By investing in our personal growth, we develop the resilience and emotional intelligence needed to navigate life's ups and downs with grace.

Moreover, personal growth extends beyond individual benefits. It has ripple effects that can positively impact our relationships, communities, and society as a whole. When we prioritise our personal growth, we become compassionate, empathetic individuals who are better equipped to understand and support others. We become agents of change, inspiring those around us to embark on their own personal growth journeys and create a collective environment that values growth and development.

In conclusion, personal growth is a vital aspect of our lives. It enables us to become self-aware, develop essential life skills, enhance our emotional well-being, and contribute to the betterment of society. By recognising and accepting the value of personal growth, we open ourselves up to a world of possibilities and opportunities for self-improvement. So, let us embrace personal growth as a life-long journey and commit ourselves to continuous learning and self-development.

Chapter 17
How to spiritually grow?

"Spiritual growth begins when you embrace the discomfort of self-reflection and surrender to the whispers of your soul"

Spiritual growth is an important aspect of personal development and self-discovery. It involves connecting with your inner self and finding meaning and purpose in life. Many individuals seek spiritual growth as a way to find peace, happiness, and fulfilment. In this chapter, we will explore some strategies and practices that can help us on our spiritual journey.

One of the key aspects of spiritual growth is self-reflection. Taking the time to look within and understand our thoughts, emotions, and beliefs is essential for personal growth. This can be done through practices such as meditation, journaling, or spending time in nature. By slowing down and creating space for introspection, we gain insight into ourselves and our place in the universe.

Another important aspect of spiritual growth is developing a sense of gratitude. By focusing on the positive aspects of our lives and expressing gratitude for the blessings we have, we cultivate a mindset of abundance and attract more positivity into our lives. This can be done through practices such as keeping a gratitude journal or simply taking a few moments each day to reflect on what we are grateful for.

In addition, connecting with others on a deeper level can greatly contribute to spiritual growth. Engaging in meaningful conversations, participating in community service, or joining a spiritual group or organisation can provide opportunities to learn from others and broaden our perspectives. By sharing our experiences, insights, and challenges with others, we not only deepen our own understanding but also contribute to the growth and wellbeing of others.

Practicing mindfulness is another powerful tool for spiritual growth. Mindfulness involves being fully present in the moment and observing our thoughts and emotions without judgment. This practice helps us develop greater self-awareness and allows us to respond to life's challenges with clarity and compassion. Mindfulness can be cultivated through practices such as meditation, yoga, or simply by incorporating small moments of mindfulness into our daily routines.

Lastly, it is important to remember that spiritual growth is a lifelong journey. It is not a destination, but rather a continuous process of growth and transformation. It requires commitment, patience, and a willingness to explore and embrace new experiences. By remaining open-minded and receptive to new ideas and perspectives, we can continue to expand our spiritual understanding and deepen our connection with ourselves and the world around us.

In conclusion, spiritual growth is a deeply personal and transformative journey. By engaging in practices such as self-reflection, gratitude, connection with others, mindfulness, and remaining open-minded, we can foster our own spiritual growth. It is through this growth that we find peace, happiness, and a sense of purpose in our lives. So let us embark on this journey with an open heart and a willingness to explore the depths of our souls.

Call To Action In This Journey Of Life

In the journey of life, there comes a time when we must take action and make a difference. It is not enough to simply exist and go through the motions. We must actively participate and contribute to the world around us. This call to action is what drives us to achieve our goals and make a meaningful impact on society.

The call to action can take many forms. It can be as simple as volunteering at a local community centre or as ambitious as starting a non-profit organisation. Whatever the action may be, the important thing is that we are actively working towards a better future.

One area where a call to action is particularly needed is in the fight against climate change. The Earth is facing unprecedented challenges, and it is up to us to address them. We must take action to reduce our carbon footprint, promote renewable energy sources, and advocate for sustainable practices. Each and every one of us has a role to play in protecting our planet for future generations.

Another area where a call to action is crucial is in the realm of social justice. There are still many injustices that persist in our society, and it is our responsibility to address them. We must speak up against racism, sexism, and any form of discrimination. We must fight for equality and ensure that everyone has access to the same opportunities and rights.

Additionally, a call to action is needed in the realm of education. Access to quality education is a fundamental right, yet many children around the world are denied this opportunity. We must work towards providing universal access to education and empowering young minds to reach their full potential. Through education, we can break the cycle of poverty and create a brighter future for all.

In conclusion, the call to action is a powerful force that drives us to make a difference in the journey of life. Whether it is in protecting the environment, promoting social justice, or improving education, we all have a role to play. We must seize the opportunity to take action and strive for a better world. Together, we can create lasting change and leave a positive legacy for future generations. The time for action is now. Will you answer the call?

Acknowledgments

To my grandmother, Florence Margery Canning, forever by my side, who I shall love until the end of my days, and beyond...

About the Author

Spirit Writer: This Journey Called "Life"

My journey commenced when I embraced my dreams and the profound messages from within. The foundation for this latest book originates from the notion that individuals often succumb to failure in pursuing their desires due to the weight of negative sentiments imposed upon them by those apprehensive about deviating from the norm.

I invite you to join me on this extraordinary quest toward attaining a deeper understanding of life's intricacies. By delving into the past and comprehending its significance, we will emerge stronger and better equipped to face whatever challenges the future may hold...

Embracing uniqueness is at the core of all my literary works, while also mustering the courage to advocate for what you truly believe in.

Look skyward and hold steadfast to your aspirations so that you can live your best life!

Wendy

facebook.com/spiritwriterspeaks

x.com/spiritwriteruk

instagram.com/healingwithspirit.co.uk

tiktok.com/spiritwriteruk

youtube.com/healingwithspirit7965

pinterest.com/spiritwriterspeaks

Printed in Great Britain
by Amazon

36650077R00040